THE BEST OF
HERMAN

THE BEST OF HERMAN®

A Herman Treasury

By Jim Unger

Andrews and McMeel
A Universal Press Syndicate Company
Kansas City

Other Popular Herman Books

The 1st Treasury of Herman
The Second Treasury of Herman
Herman, The Third Treasury
Herman: The Fourth Treasury
Herman Treasury 5
Herman: The Sixth Treasury
Herman Over the Wall: The Seventh Treasury
Herman VIII

"The key to happiness and freedom is a sense of humor and a sense of humor is nothing more or less than the ability to laugh at oneself."

—Jim Unger, from *The 1st Treasury of Herman*

"To be honest, I'd heard you'd gone abroad."

They wanted me to do another book of cartoons. I told them I would write something for a change. It'll give me a chance to clear up some of the mystery.

There's a big difference between thinking, writing, and talking. I sometimes look at some of my old cartoons and even I can't understand the gag! In fact, I can't even remember where the "incident" was supposed to be taking place! Totally baffled, I sit there wondering what I must have been thinking.

When I became self-employed I think I hired the wrong person.

"Okay, you've got five minutes to capture my interest."

"This is the third time you've been back in a week. Why don't you wear a tee-shirt?"

"You're not Robert Redford."

"For crying out loud! If it's that important to you, take the afternoon off."

"You know, if you keep telling me about birds and bees, I'm gonna lose interest in girls."

"The results of your tests were negative. Get lost!"

"I've changed my mind. I'll have a cheese sandwich."

"Herman ... two is load ... THREE is fire!"

"Is it still raining?"

"I don't wanna be a juror!
Can't I be a witness?"

"Just take a seat, son. You're next."

"Hey, Harry! Look at this guy's wife."

"All bets are off if you don't quit laughing."

"Two sets to love is not the end of the world, you know!"

"I'm trying to sleep. What have you got up here—a performing elephant?"

"What's so dumb about cutting out a full-page advertisement?"

"Listen, I've got to go. Give my love to everyone in Australia."

"D'you realize we've been out for four hours and we're not even on the third green?"

"Hey you. I'm trying to watch television."

"Are you eating properly and getting plenty of exercise?"

"Stay calm ... I'm gonna get a second opinion on your blood pressure."

"It says here you're intelligent, honest and reliable. What makes you think you'd be an asset to this company?"

"Shall I turn it off?"

"Sure it's big, but it'll do an average room in three minutes."

"If you remember, I did mention possible side-effects."

"Okay, take a break!"

"I GOT A HOLE-IN-ONE!"

"I was cleaning it!"

"Mommy had this kitchen custom built."

"The artist, knowing that beauty is perceived in the eye of the beholder, strives by whatever means, to broaden the perception of others in the hope that they will share his joy."

—Jim Unger, from *The Second Herman Treasury*

"Don't forget to mark it 'Personal.'"

"I hope it tastes good. I'm boiling
your socks."

"My wife's on her way up, Gladys;
so you're my new secretary and
Francine's going for an early lunch."

HERMAN

JIM Unger

I'M NOT JUST ANOTHER PRETTY FACE.

IF I'M ELECTED, I INTEND TO SLASH TAXES BY 75%.

VOTE FOR

REVITALIZE.....

VOTE FOR

IT'S 10.A.M...

VOTE FOR

YOU'RE READING THE 2 O'CLOCK SPEECH.

VOTE FOR

AND....DOUBLE EXISTING OLD-AGE PENSIONS.... AND PROVIDE FREE HEALTH CARE.

E FOR

"There goes my tip, right?"

"Members of the jury, I ask you—does my client look like a man of violence?"

"Your wife took the new baby home in a cab an hour ago."

"If there was another man in my life, do you honestly think I'd be sitting here?"

"FIRED! Does that mean I won't get the raise?"

"Want me to get you a shopping cart?"

"Your plane's been delayed ten minutes. A couple of rivets popped loose."

"D'you get the feeling one of us is getting ripped off?"

"Don't blame me. I was cleaning his cage and he flew up the pipe."

"Did you feel the earthquake?"

"Dentistry's come a long way in the last few years."

"You're washing the floor with tomorrow's soup-of-the-day!"

"Is that everything, just a bar of soap?"

"You phoned me and said you had amnesia; don't you remember?"

"Here, don't touch the stick."

"Pretend you're a purse snatcher. I wanna try something."

"There! Aren't you glad I made you wear your seat belt?"

"He's never flown before!"

"Why don't you start going to bed earlier?"

"They said something about five thousand UFOs landing in Idaho, then cut to a commercial."

"Don't you want your receipt?"

HERMAN by Jim Unger

HE JUST WON $5,000.

I AUDITIONED FOR A TV GAME SHOW ONCE.

WHAT HAPPENED?

I WAS REJECTED.

YOU KNOW WHEN THEY SHOW A CLOSE-UP OF YOUR FACE.....

...AND READ OUT ALL THE PRIZES YOU COULD WIN...

THEY SAID I DIDN'T LOOK EXCITED ENOUGH.

**"They knew how to build skeletons
in those days."**

**"Why take a week off? You've got time to
get married and have a honeymoon on one
of your coffee breaks."**

"Did you sleep okay, Herman?"

"Instead of taking me to an expensive dinner, can I have the money?"

"Ambulance or not, Sunshine, *you* left the scene of an accident."

"Do you want the 75 cents or not?"

"Whadda you think of gun control?"

"Have you decided?"

"I told you not to wear that dumb hat."

"Haven't you got a brush?"

"You left your wallet at the fish shop!"

"Use your fingers."

"Doc, it's a marvelous idea! You fill 'em up
with flu vaccine and put them on all the chairs
in your waiting room."

"I know you take a shower almost every day.
You almost took one Monday, you almost took
one Tuesday……"

"I claim this planet in the name of
Bluggrovia."

"I thought TV was supposed to make you violent!"

"When are you gonna understand? We're not 'jet-set' we're 'train-set.'"

"Of course your operation is 'absolutely necessary.' Without it I don't get a summer vacation."

"I don't know how you manage to eat all my cooking and never put on any weight."

"Don't let them see the frying pan!"

"What do I have to do to get some service around here?"

"He watched a heart transplant on TV three days ago, and he's still recovering."

"This one's called, 'Bowl of Fruit on Very High Table.'"

"The main thing with a horse is you've got to make sure he knows who's the boss."

"STAMPEDE!"

"Can't you get on with your work without watching me all the time?"

"We only have to empty it once a month."

"It is OK if I scream with agony between answering the questions?"

"He won't eat."

"Reductionism" in science means reducing things down to their smallest elements in an attempt to understand them. In a way, that's like trying to understand the Pacific Ocean by studying the sex organs of a shrimp. You can only go so far with it.

A cartoonist is a "reductionist." Reducing people, places, and things down to basic fundamentals can be both revealing and sometimes quite startling.

"You in one of your moods again?"

"You wait! As soon as someone discovers gravity, they'll all come down and hit the ground."

"You come 50 million miles and all you can tell me is, 'Stick that meat on the fire; it'll taste better'?"

"You asked us to build a computer which could replace the government."

HERMAN

JIM Unger

I'M NOT LOOKING FORWARD TO IT....

YOU KNOW WHAT MEN ARE LIKE.

WHEN I GO HOME TOMORROW, THERE'LL BE A PILE OF DIRTY DISHES IN THE SINK.

MY HUSBAND'S NOT LIKE THAT.

HE'S VERY CONSIDERATE WHEN I'M AWAY.

... EATS RIGHT OUT OF THE CANS.

"I've got the results of your X-rays."

"Mom found your credit cards under the mattress and she's gone shopping."

"The TV won't be ready 'til next Friday."

"Look, as soon as a private room becomes available, you'll get one."

"That's the fifth time you've wished me a Merry Christmas. What are you up to?"

"Ask him if he ever heard of a tortoise having a heart attack."

"Start? Start what? I thought you said you hired me to take care of the books."

"It just says, 'Windows repaired—five bucks.'"

"That one's automatic!"

"I know you've been late for work twice this week. I still think it's stupid to sleep in the car!"

"Whaddyer mean, it's a model? How much bigger d'you wanna build it?"

"How was Africa?"

"Have a good vacation. I've decided not to give you your bad news until you get back."

"It's a *grocery* list, Brother Clarence!"

"I think we had much nicer diseases when I was a girl."

"It's me. I'm changing my image."

"I don't care if it is plastic. I could have had a heart attack."

"If I don't get a pay-raise soon, I'm gonna blow the lid off this crummy zoo."

"Mr. Henderson will see you now."

**"Thanks for doing my homework last night.
The teacher thinks I'm retarded!"**

HERMAN

JIM Unger

"When we get home, pretend you're out of breath."

"Dennis is a sweet, sensitive guy, and if you don't let us get married he's gonna break both your legs."

"Herman fixed the washer!"

"Everything's cut-and-dried with you isn't it? Even baby-sitting!"

"Meadows, the doctor says I need more exercise, so I want you to start jogging for me."

"Kid, it's against the law to tell people you're 50 years old."

"If you insist on laughing, sir, I must ask you to browse in the humor section."

"Make sure you hand that pass back before you leave the building."

"If you don't go to sleep, you're gonna be practicing that swing in a wheelchair."

"I've unclogged the upstairs bath."

"Have what you like up to $1.50."

"I'll explain later. He had to go to the hospital."

"How are you getting on with the diet?"

"Hidden camera commercial, take 9."

"Does that hurt?"

"Dearly beloved, as this is John's third wedding and Betty's second, I'll make this as brief as possible."

"Today's diet, 'Twiggy.' One spoonful of peas and half a carrot."

"I know you want to play Hamlet, but for this one television commercial you're a stick of celery."

"Keep out! Keep out! K-E-E-P O-U-T."

"Move over a bit. I can't see the Grand Canyon."

"I'll take a check if you've got identification."

"Did you remember to bring my suntan oil?"

"When you told me on the phone you were 42, 22, 38 I didn't realize you meant your age, your I.Q., and your shoe size."

"You ordered a small Pisa."

"You've got Egyptian flu. You're going to be a 'mummy.'"

"Any twit can win a hole with 22 lucky shots."

"Your account is $28 overdrawn."

"When they invented the first clock, how did they know what time to set it?"

"Get me a lawyer."

Imagine if you had been born in a completely different country. You would probably speak a different language and have a different religion. You'd like different people, different foods. Maybe you'd hate all the people you now like. In short, you'd be a completely different person but it would still be "you."

"How long have you had your feet on the wrong legs?"

"The reason meat is expensive is because no one ever argued with a guy holding one of these."

"It's called 'Pigeons Beware.'"

"Maybe you're beginning to get the message that we need a recreation room."

by Jim Unger

OKAY... ONE LAST TIME...

TENT... SLEEPING BAGS... MATCHES... CHOCOLATE.. ICE CREAM...SALAMI... PICKLES...

MAPS... SPAGHETTI... COMPASS... COOKIES... SPOONS.. ASSORTED NUTS.. BREAD..CHEESE..

I HOPE WE HAVEN'T FORGOTTEN ANYTHING.

IF ANYONE NEEDS ME FOR A COUPLE OF MONTHS...I'LL BE OUT IN THE BACK YARD.

"I wanted to leave you a tip but I haven't got change for a quarter."

"They said he wasn't to leave the office 'til the books balanced."

"I can promise you I wake up at the slightest sound."

"Let me guess. She gave you your money back."

"You've got an hour to paint your nails and an hour to talk to your mother. I'm going to a meeting."

"I'm sure he'll be sorry he missed you."

"For a guy who writes his diary a month in advance, yes, I'd say you were in a rut."

"That's the second time you've fallen asleep in the bath with your mouth open."

"I told them they could watch 'til theirs was fixed."

"I see you finally sewed on my button!"

"Did you say this pizza gave you indigestion?"

"Four months, eight days, five hours and twenty minutes. Four months, eight days, five hours and nineteen minutes."

"Hospital regulations. You gotta wear the straps while I read the bill."

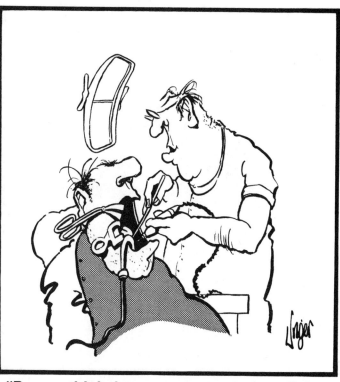

"Do you think the current economic policies will do anything to ease the overall unemployment picture and dampen inflation?"

"I cut a piece off the bottom and patched your shirt."

"Butcher Harris is doing this one tomorrow morning."

"'F' means 'fantastic.'"

"I'm NOT going camping. If you wanna get back to nature, take the bug screen out of the window for half an hour."

"You've got six wives waiting for you on the outside. Are you sure you want a parole?"

"This watch you bought me is a great conversation piece. I have to ask everybody the time!"

**"I'll have to X-ray your arm again.
This one is overexposed."**

HERMAN

JIM

WE'RE ON THE CUTTING EDGE.

...RANGE OF 800 MILES.

YOU CAN PICK ANY SPOT ON THE MAP.

NO MORE LANDFILLS...

AND I CAN GET AS MANY AS YOU WANT.

STRIPPED DOWN, IT TAKES 40 TONS OF GARBAGE, ONE WAY.

"You're sure I'll be able to swim with it?"

"Are you sure you're comfortable?"

"Is this your first blind date?"

"Congratulations! He seems very bright."

"Whose turn was it to put the stupid dog out last night?"

"Well, if a fool and his money are soon parted, who's got yours?"

"As I remember, you always were a big kid for your age."

"Okay, I'm coming out now. Close your eyes!"

"Boy, Harry, you sure look different without your wallet!"

"You can't be expected to get it right the first time!"

"Next time you go to the store, get some proper paper napkins."

"If you don't learn a trade, how are you going to know what kind of work you're out of?"

"The way you carry on, you'd think I enjoy these business trips."

"I wanted a steady worker. You're absolutely motionless."

"I'm telling you; you haven't got a complex. You're downright inferior."

"...and don't call me illiterate. My Ma and Pa have been married for thirty-eight years."

75

"Is that the way you normally stand?"

"The Marquis of Halifax writes, 'The vanity of teaching doth oft tempt man to forget he is a blockhead.'"

"I said we ought to iron out our differences so she hit me with the steam iron."

"I see you've fixed the drip!"

"Set the clock for 5:30!"

"FORE."

"As I see it, you've got a choice between a 'birdie' and promotion to branch manager."

"Memorize this, it's your New Year's resolutions."

"GET OFF THAT OILY MAN WITH YOUR BEST SHOES ON."

"If you're coming ashore buddy, I wanna see your passport."

"Here, you wanted a shark's-tooth necklace. Dig those outa my leg."

"Leave the car keys just in case something grabs you out there."

"I hope you know your stuff.
I'm a very weak swimmer."

"When are you gonna start facing reality?"

I've heard people say it's bad grammar to use words like "gonna." It's not bad grammar, it's another word and very often it's funnier than "going to."... It adds to the language.

Another "word" to a writer is another color to a painter.

Some people complain about the way others abuse the language by saying the opposite of what they mean. Something described as "bad" means it's "good." How shameful! Polite society has learned to accept phrases like "awfully nice of you" and "terribly sweet of you."

"That must have been one heavy suitcase!"

"What's jet lag? I think I've got it."

"A truck ran over my cast!"

"For the tenth time, I'm NOT going bowling."

"If you're so dead-set against gambling, how come you're still in the marriage business?"

"Look what your stupid uncle gave us. What d'yer think it is?"

"Debbie looks exactly like me when I was 18."

"For Pete's sake, don't sit behind her when we get inside."

"I dunno why you love nature after what it did to you."

"We can't elope. I haven't got a suitcase."

"Well, well, my secret file tells me that since 1948 this is your grandmother's seventh funeral."

"What about our religious differences? I worship money and you're broke!"

"I see you've listed your hobbies as alpine skiing, scuba diving, skydiving, treasure hunting and climbing Mount Everest."

"Will you shove off? I'm sick of your jealousy!"

"Where do you think you get off taking out your own appendix?"

"You dropped it. You get it!"

"I told you I was smart. My teacher says she's given up trying to teach me anything."

"He thinks we're muggers!"

"Stop whining. I caught it so I'll carry it."

"I thought that clown had fixed the fridge."

"Hey, Tex. Come and settle an argument.
Is this arrow Apache or Sioux?"

"Maturity is a feeling that comes over you
when you look back on your life and realize
you were wrong on just about everything."

"Don't go rushing into marriage. Look around
for a couple of years like your mother did."

"What exactly is 'new, improved lettuce?'"

"It went around twice and stopped on 18."

"HIPPY!"

"He wants a blue dress for his wife, size 'fat.'"

"Are you taking your bikini?"

**"We need a bicycle built for two—
and one for me."**

by Jim Unger

I SEE YOU'RE BACK...

HOW'S YOUR HUSBAND?

I DON'T KNOW HOW MUCH MORE I CAN TAKE OF HIM!

WE SPENT THREE HOURS DOWN AT THE HOSPITAL BECAUSE HE WOKE UP WITH RED LUMPS AND BLOTCHES ALL OVER HIS CHIN AND NECK.

BLOTCHES!

WHAT WAS IT?

SPAGHETTI SAUCE.

"I told her I wanted a 'trial separation' so she tried to separate my shoulder!"

"Look at this! You give those mice an inch and they take a mile!"

"I'm not the world's greatest cook, but I think you'll enjoy my cornflakes."

"You can't afford to get married on the salary I'm paying you—and one day you'll thank me."

"I'll have to open you up again; that watch
has great sentimental value."

"Want me to get you a wig for your birthday?"

"You only want me to get a haircut because
you're jealous."

"I know your landlord depends on the rent,
but you still can't list him as a dependent."

"He's probably taking a breather on his way north."

"The 50-cent surcharge is for the clean fork I brought you when you dropped the other one."

"I hope you used warm water. I don't want to listen to those things chattering all night."

"Where's the kids?"

"I'm not gonna take any coffee breaks this week so I can have Friday off."

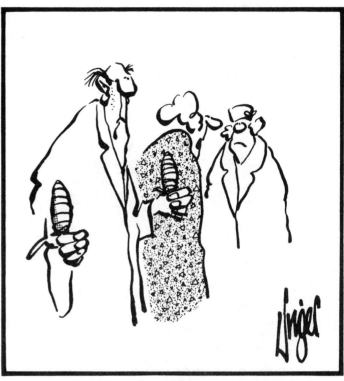

"I was showing my sister-in-law how I slammed his thumb in the car door."

"Got any 'get sick' cards?"

"I told you not to order 'home fries!' The chef lives 20 miles away."

"You're not supposed to just pour the stew into the lunch pail."

"If you're right about women changing after they get married, I'm in luck! My fiancée can't cook and she argues every five minutes."

"Grannie, your horoscope says be prepared for a whirlwind romance!"

"I haven't understood one word you said. Come back when your face gets better."

"I lost 10 pounds once. To be honest,
I didn't notice any difference."

"Is he allowed to play with knives?
He's cut my hose!"

"I told him he could have your 'left-overs.'"

"If you get up a little earlier, you'd have more time to shave!"

"You wasted all day taking this film and it's blank."

"I wish you'd let me know you were coming in here. I had to throw away a perfectly good frozen dinner."

"How come God put all the vitamins in cabbage and nothing in candy?"

"The computer says it'll probably try to stick that rubber thing in your mouth."

Have you ever watched people dancing on TV with the sound turned off?

Imagine coming here from another planet with no comprehension of sound. You'd think you were in a madhouse. I feel like that sometimes. I'm missing the music somewhere.

"Mother, I thought we'd agreed—
'no luxuries.'"

"It's a whole different world down there."

"Your doctor wants to marry me if you
don't make it."

HERMAN

BY: JIM UNGER

"Wake up. The cat's got your teeth."

"If you want a concise professional opinion: You're as nutty as a fruitcake."

"Operator, how do I make a long-distance call from here?"

"Where did you get these eggs?"

"I'll give you something for gas!"

"You got nothing to smile about."

"Don't move while I'm gone.
You'll spill my drink."

"I phoned the doctor. You're supposed to get plenty of fluids."

"It's okay! I found the keys."

"You the guy who called a plumber?"

"I wish you hadn't worn that tie. It doesn't go with your jacket."

"This looks good—'Mailman flavored.'"

"This is the latest exerciser. It's an inflatable mother-in-law and a baseball bat!"

"I warned you about iron tonic. Your stomach's rusty."

"If I didn't have all my faults, I wouldn't have had to marry a creep like you."

"This idiot opened all the windows halfway through the car wash."

"Look at that! 62 years old and not a single cavity."

"When he was six years old, my father was kidnapped by headhunters and never seen again."

"They don't give us time to learn anything; we have to listen to the teacher all day."

"Don't turn around, and hand over the keys to the monkey house."

MY POOR SISTER....

THAT STANLEY IS SO CHEAP.... MY SISTER LOST HER CREDIT CARD AND HE WON'T GET HER ANOTHER ONE BECAUSE HE SAYS SHE SPENDS TOO MUCH.

ANYWAY, SHE SURE TAUGHT HIM A LESSON TODAY..... SHE WENT OUT AND BOUGHT A STACK OF NEW CLOTHES FOR HERSELF AND THE KIDS...

..NEW CARPETS...STEREO...THE WHOLE WORKS.....HE'S IN FOR ONE BIG SURPRISE NEXT MONTH..

HOW DID SHE MANAGE THAT?

WHAT?

HOW DID SHE MANAGE TO BUY ALL THAT STUFF WITHOUT A CREDIT CARD?

I LENT HER MINE.

111

"We got a nice postcard from those little green guys in the U.F.O."

"Ignorance of the law is no excuse, buddy."

"Can you fix them by Saturday? I'm in the finals."

"It says, 'Your day will be greatly influenced by the planet Neptune.'"

"I'm sorry, sir, you'll have to return to your seat. We'll be landing in a few minutes."

"Your hat's full of cigarette butts again!"

"Who d'you think wants to drink that after *you've* been sitting in it?"

"WAIST EIGHTY-TWO."

"I'm sorry, we're out of 'Multivitamins Plus Iron.'"

"George thinks they should consider releasing a few human beings back into the wild."

"You know I don't keep bath crystals in the kitchen. This is Jell-O powder!"

"That's the last time we'll use this hospital!"

"They said you were wearing this when you fell off the roof."

"Gimme a gin and lettuce."

"He painted that one on our camping trip."

"We're looking for someone honest, hardworking, and totally devoid of ambition."

"Your honor, if my client is found not guilty, he could lose more than $2 million in book royalties alone."

"She coulda been Miss Universe on any other planet."

"I can start work on Monday if I don't win the lottery."

"Don't drive around like that! Find a gas station!"

"HOLD IT."

"What accident? I told you I was making bookends."

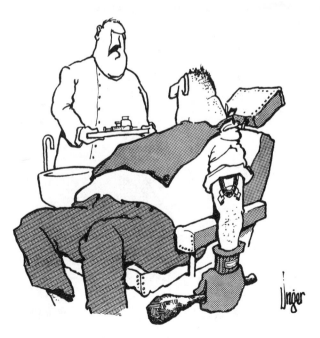

"Don't worry, this'll probably hurt me more than you."

"If I can't afford to buy a really expensive birthday gift, I don't buy anything at all. So I didn't get you anything."

"Where do I put my mouth?"

"These fireplace logs are just pieces of a tree. Haven't you got any of the real plastic ones?"

"Port-starboard-port-starboard. Can't you speak English?"

"You can sit there 'til I find out where you hid my glasses!"

"You sure that's beef?"

At first glance, the unmolested natural world appears much more beautiful than us "humans," but the reasons are not all bad. The human race has developed "morality." We have learned to care.

You don't see a lot of wheelchairs trailing along at the back of a herd of zebras.

If a zebra named Maurice wakes up one morning with a cramp in his leg, hundreds of pairs of eyes are watching his every move. All the other zebras are thinking they're going to have a quiet day if they stay away from Maurice and the lions and vultures start moving in a little closer. Let's face it, most of us would have been gone long ago.

"Make sure you get one with a roof-rack."

"It'll go away if you don't keep looking at it."

"It looked smaller in the store!"

HERMAN

BY: JIM UNGER

"DID YOU SEE THIS?"

"IT SAYS HERE THAT 98% OF ALL FIRST OFFENDERS ATTENDED SOME SCHOOL...."

"...97% HAD TIGHT SHOES AS A CHILD."

"94% PARENTS QUARRELED."

"92% HAD SOME RELIGIOUS TRAINING."

"86% READ PORNOGRAPHY."

"85% LIVED WITH AN INCESSANT TALKER."

123

"You always said you liked it strong."

"Why do you always decide to take a bath just when supper's ready?"

"Think it'll work?"

"He says it's no use. He's GOTTA do it."

"His doctor told him to cut out sugar."

"I hate to mention it, but there was $1.80
on the meter when I hit that truck."

"I know $17 is a lot of money, but diamonds
are forever!"

"Hey, poodle ... sweetheart. ...
How's it going, baby?"

"Did you or did you not tell him I was a Homo sapiens?"

"They're all the same . ... As soon as I laid the egg, he was off."

"Will you turn that fan down!"

"What exactly do you mean, Doc, by 'your blood pressure pills aren't working?'"

"I can't go out tonight, Frank;
I'm washing my hair."

"I'd know your scrawl anywhere, you creep!"

"Maybe next time you'll think twice about
losing your key."

"Why don't you let your husband go to
the ball game?"

"No one said the job was gonna be a bed of roses."

"Is it too spicy?"

"Will ya get a move on."

"Folks, the main reason you're not getting a good picture is because you bought yourselves a microwave oven."

"So this is Dotty, your wife."

"Did you knock?"

"QUIT SHOVING!"

"Well, you knew we had only one tree when you bought it."

"Don't tell me your mother's coming to dinner!"

"Did you shake the bottle?"

"I think you'll find, sir, our brochure says 'safe beach.' You must have gone into the water."

"Hello, Frank. Does my insurance cover me for snapped off needles?"

"Your mother's been at my wine again."

"You say you spent five years at the North Pole?"

"You gonna be long? I'm double-parked."

"It was yesterday."

"How can I find anything when you keep leaving this razor all over the bathroom?"

"If you want to leave, Maxine, I won't stand in your way."

"Your honor, my client is the product of a broken home."

"I think you'll find my test results are a pretty good indication of your abilities as a teacher."

"Is that what they teach you at mailman's college?"

"They say you get what you pay for: It cost me four bucks to get married."

"It's a big step—getting married. You'll have to give me some time to think about it. What was your name again?"

"What's the matter with you? Can't you save that for during the commercials?"

"… and cancel the tickets to Acapulco."

"Sorry, pal, you can't come in here with a tie."

"He took out my appendix and I haven't got a scar."

"Stay away from that cake in the fridge."

"I may have to ruin your coat."

"OK, five more minutes, then we'll go somewhere else."

"My husband spent all weekend trying to fix it."

"Take one of these out every four hours."

"Don't get me any more of this roll-on deodorant."

"We had to remove your brain for a couple of days, so just try to relax."

It's possible the universe is creating its own brain, its own "thinking process." Not so strange when you remember that all living things are made up of trillions of other things and yet each appears to be animated by one "mind."

"To me, life is like an orchard. You pick the fruit when you see it. For years, I bummed around the world looking for happiness. Then one day I realized happiness isn't something you find. All the happiness in the world is between your own two ears."

—Jim Unger, from *Herman, The Third Treasury*

HERMAN

BY: JIM UNGER

"He gets those sudden migraines."

"Why don't you read the rotten map yourself!"

"Do I look stupid? Of course you can marry my daughter."

"Makes you wonder how we ever managed without it."

"I just wanted to tell you I'm gonna be late."

"What have you got within walking distance?"

"If I do happen to pick him out, what are the chances of his being held in custody long enough for me to emigrate?"

"I could have left you a tip if you hadn't talked me into that cheesecake."

"I asked my new secretary to get me a sheet of graph paper."

"It's just till I fix the hole in our fence."

"I think you've had enough. Why don't I call you a cab?"

"Imagine anyone planting a tree right there!"

"Fish and chips and forty-two chef's salads."

"If I was a tipper, you'd definitely get one."

"I've quit my job at the bank."

"How does anyone get four aces six times in a row?"

"I left the circus 17 years ago and I think I still miss it!"

"Did they tell you I had to take one of my pills at 2 o'clock?"

"Show me what to press if I want to record a movie after I've gone to bed."

**"The wife used to do quite a bit of modeling
...until she lost her tube of glue."**

by Jim Unger

IT'S YOUR NEPHEW, REGGIE.

YOU SHOULD LISTEN TO YOUR UNCLE... WHEN YOU GET TO HIS AGE, YOU LEARN A THING OR TWO.

HE'S JOINED THE NAVY.

THEY OFFERED ME A COMMISSION.

DON'T TAKE IT...

TELL 'EM YOU WANT A REGULAR WAGE.

"You have to do your own dishes."

"Have you done the north slope?"

"You'll be pleased to know, madame, we just landed safely at the international airport."

"My cousin, Irene, knows a good lawyer."

"If I pay this amount of taxes, I'll qualify for tax exemption as a nonprofit organization!"

"Mr. Picasso, I'll be able to work only a half-day Thursday."

"Get me to the airport in 10 minutes and I *may* overlook this filthy cab."

"I gotta leave you on your own for a few weeks."

"It's for my mother-in-law.
Got anything rabid?"

"He loves people. But mostly he gets
canned dog food."

"It's an emergency. She's gotta be at the
hairdresser in three minutes."

"This beef Wellington tastes like rubber boots!"

"We got any *white* salmon?"

"So this is your private box at the theater!"

"I wanna say, 'take your job and shove it' in poinsettias."

"He thinks a chiropractor is an
Egyptian doctor."

"I'll give you directions. Just don't drive
above jogging speed."

"He had an emergency operation."

"I get a real deal on fire insurance."

"If she doesn't show, d'yer wanna come to Niagara Falls?"

"My ex-husband was up all night buying everybody drinks."

"The honeymoon suite is booked for another 20 minutes."

"We went to Greece for a second honeymoon. Six days and seven fights."

"It'll speed things up if you order the meatloaf."

"My life insurance company has offered me a reduction if I eat out."

"Your cut in salary is a cost-of-living adjustment due to the falling price of coffee."

"I don't want a son-in-law who's stupid enough to marry my daughter."

"It's no use. I can't sleep with
this wallpaper."

"Hang on, there's a guy here complaining about the bus being overcrowded."

D'you remember the story about the blind men trying to describe the elephant they were touching. One felt its leg and said it was like a tree. Another, grabbing its trunk said it was like a snake.

Did you ever wonder what the other blind men must have been thinking, waiting for their turn to speak? They must have thought the others were crazy.

Maybe that's why we all think everybody else in the world is crazy except us, because "truth" and "reality" are like that elephant. And everyone has a very personal piece of it.

Humor helps us to realize how much alike we really are.

HERMAN

BY: JIM UNGER

MAY I BE VERY BLUNT.

MY BOY IS ONLY 18 YEARS OLD.

HIS MOTHER AND I HAVE TOLD HIM ALL ABOUT THE "YOU-KNOW-WHAT."

BIRDS AND BEES AND ALL THAT MALARKEY.

.THE THINGAMAJIG AND THE WHAT'S-IT.

SO WHY DOES HE NEED SEX EDUCATION IN SCHOOL?

"Her sister's making 10 bucks a week."

"You're exactly the same size as me."

"Table for two. Food for five."

"He's not very sociable."

"Your baggage arrived, but your wife went to Tokyo."

"You'll be hearing from my lawyer."

"That's guaranteed waterproof to 100 fathoms."

"They're specially bred for long walks."

"Here's your supper. I've waxed the floor."

"He sure looks forward to your weekly visits."

"This one was driven by a little old lady and her nephew."

"Extraterrestrials have landed."

"What are you here for?"

"It took me three hours, but I finally discovered why you're limping. You lost the heel off your shoe."

"How much longer you gonna be in this bathroom?"

"Have you got a smoke alarm I can switch off while I'm cooking?"

"Remember six years ago when you left the gate open?"

"Terrible thing, depression."

"I've decided to try shock treatment."

"Are you coming hunting, or are you gonna sit around here all day inventing?"

HERE'S A NEWS BULLETIN...

DUE TO A BREAKDOWN IN SALARY NEGOTIATIONS...

DUE TO A BREAKDOWN IN SALARY NEGOTIATIONS...

BETWEEN MYSELF AND THIS NETWORK...

BETWEEN MYSELF AND THIS NETWORK...

AFTER NINE YEARS...

AND MUCH SOUL-SEARCHING...

I'VE DECIDED TO QUIT MY JOB!

171

"Does he bite?"

"Where do you want the TV?"

"If you don't keep quiet I'm gonna phone
all your friends and tell them how
old you really are."

"Okay, now shift your weight onto the left leg
during the follow-through."

"I had a good job waiting for me on the outside, but they installed a burglar alarm."

"Now don't worry about the noise this drill makes."

"If I had to guess, I'd say a very large horsefly."

"Bagel!"

"You won't find it under 'plumber.'
Look under 'drain surgeon.'"

"We the jury find the defendant not guilty
by reason of insanity."

"I thought it was you."

"How often do you find a basement
apartment with a balcony?"

"I like it fairly short and parted in the middle."   **"You won't find a job in the Sports section!"**

**"You say you were inside robbing the bank
and someone stole your car?"**

**"D'you mind if I take a photo? It's not often
we get a 15-cent tip."**

"I'm fixing up the room. Her mother's coming to stay with us for a week."

"Is it my fault if the foreman at my last place started a fight?"

"You heard me! Did I say 'rice' or 'dice?'"

"No, it's not easy putting nine adopted kids through college on 80 smackers a week!"

"What's it like for cornering?"

"We just don't see eye to eye anymore."

"Quit fooling around!"

"We're not too happy with the caterers."

"Is this allowed?"

"He stole $15 million, your honor, and he wants to plead 'guilty with an explanation.'"

"I don't think I'll bother with a tan
'til I get out."

"If my dad asks you what you do for a living, say you're a marine biologist!"

"It looks better in the other room."

"I can do shorthand! It just takes a little longer."

"There's four clean socks in here. One blue, one brown, one green, and one red."

"Forget the facelift. I think we'll try lowering your body."

"My mistake! I thought I heard a noise down here."

"You're looking a lot better today, Ralph."

"Visiting hours are 2 'til 4 p.m."

HERMAN

JIM

"Got any wide-bottom shirts?"

"Why did you move your plate?"

"I can get a court order to stop you from teaching her to cook."

"LADIES AND GENTLEMEN, the bride and groom!"

"Got any books on dog training?"

"No wonder your brother never writes!"

"No, you can't wear it to school.
Put it back on the wall."

"I can't remember the last time you put your
arm around me at the movies."

"Socks again! I bought you a digital watch."

"Let's see. How much rent do you owe me with 17 hotels on Boardwalk?"

"I'm charging you a dollar for whatever it is you've got in your mouth."

"Take a seat. It'll be about two days."

"I'm only really happy when I'm miserable."

"I warned you about pulling out gray hairs."

"Are you sure it's dead?"

"You can call me apathetic if you like.
See how much I care."

"I'm sorry, sir. You said you wanted the cheapest room."

"Have you heard that expression, 'You are what you eat?'"

"I had to give everyone *their money back*!"

"I'm studying astrophysics and you're reading me 'Goldilocks and the Three Bears'!"

"This one just says *Fold.*"

HERMAN

BY: JIM UNGER

LIFE'S A MYSTERY.

I JUST DON'T GET IT...

YOU BOUGHT YOUR WIFE AN $800 DISHWASHER.

I BOUGHT MINE A BOTTLE OF DISHWASHING LIQUID.

I CAN'T FIGURE OUT WHAT I DID WITH THE $798.

"I don't know what this is, but you need a new one."

"I don't want to worry you, but the guy who delivered the pizza was your financial planner."

"I don't think Mom makes spaghetti on toast like that."

"This is my nephew, Eric. He wants to borrow that $100 you still owe me."

"Today's special is spaghetti with alphabet letters in the sauce."

"Size what?"

"That's just his way of saying he wants you to stay!"

"I wish I could think of a way of eliminating this static cling."

"You can't blame TV if you're dumb enough to walk up to a 300-lb. truck driver and say, 'Ring around the collar.'"

"We implant this behind your left ear and you won't even know it's there."

"Look at my rug! I told you not to put exploding cheese down the mouseholes."

"You'll get used to that! A fireman lives upstairs."

"This rascal chased the wife's mother
20 feet up a tree."

"Supper ready?"

"Your wife is still under the anesthetic
and from what I've heard, this would
be a good time to see her."

"Quit griping! D'you want your windows
washed or not?"

"You better make sure I get it back Friday."

"Who do you think's gonna drink that?"

"How come my photo's got all these little holes in it?"

"Joe's my bodyguard till I tell you where I've been all night."

"Why don't you listen? I said bring me a WENCH."

"You had a hair transplant?"

"Whaddyer mean I should have told you? I told you weeks ago."

"What are you asking me for?"

"How did things go down at the old divorce court?"

"The doctor won't be long. Are you sure you wouldn't like a cup of coffee?"

"We'll have to have dinner out; the toaster's broken."

"Can the police give you a speeding ticket in a car wash?"

"How do you expect me to average 55 miles an hour if I don't speed?"

"Show me that piece of paper again with the calculations on it."

"I keep going hot and cold."

"Well, the window's open. I hope you're satisfied."

"Would you believe it? I've been all over town trying to get you some flowers."

"Gee Ralph, the party was yesterday!"

"Here ... tell your mother we're out.
She won't believe me."

"I told you not to drink all that coffee."

"I told you last week I had to work
late tonight!"

"Thirty-five thousand feet, one way."

"I hope you're not one of those people who has trouble swallowing pills."

"Do you mind telling me why there are carpet fibers on this sausage?"

"You know what they say, 'Two can starve as cheaply as one.'"

"I would've been here sooner but our iceberg hit a ship."

Albert Einstein once said that if he had to choose between "knowledge" and "imagination," he would choose "imagination." That's probably why he smiled a lot.

"This wildlife book you sold me is nothing but animals!"

THE END